Music from the Video Game

The SIMS™

ISBN 978-1-70517-909-3

HAL•LEONARD®
——— A Muse Group Company ———

Visit Hal Leonard Online at
www.halleonard.com

World headquarters, contact:
Hal Leonard
7777 West Bluemound Road
Milwaukee, WI 53213
Email: info@halleonard.com

In Europe, contact:
Hal Leonard Europe Limited
Dettingen Way
Bury St Edmunds, Suffolk, IP33 3YB
Email: info@halleonardeurope.com

In Australia, contact:
Hal Leonard Australia Pty. Ltd.
4 Lentara Court
Cheltenham, Victoria, 3192 Australia
Email: info@halleonard.com.au

BARE BONES

from THE SIMS 2

By MARK MOTHERSBAUGH

BUSY SIM
from THE SIMS 2

By MARK MOTHERSBAUGH

To Coda ⊕

D.C. al Coda
(with repeat)

CODA
⊕

BUYING LUMBER

from THE SIMS

By JERRY MARTIN

Slowly and freely

FIRST VOLLEY
from THE SIMS 2

By MARK MOTHERSBAUGH

GROCERIES

from THE SIMS

By MARC RUSSO

D.S. al Coda

CODA

IT'S THE SIMS

from THE SIMS 4

By ILAN ESHKERI

With energy

MAKEOVER

from THE SIMS 2

By MARK MOTHERSBAUGH

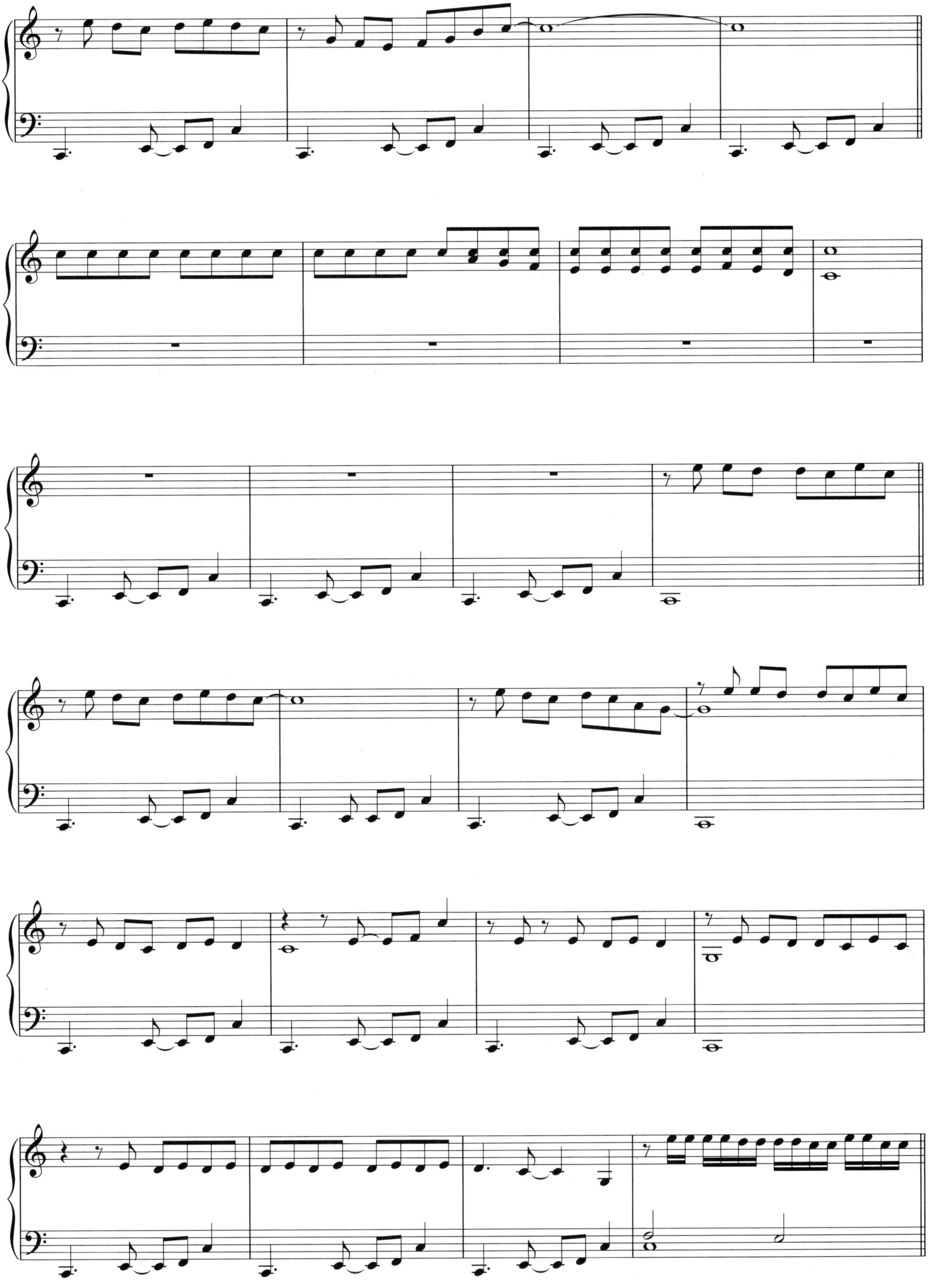

24

2nd time, D.S. al Coda

CODA

MALL RAT

from THE SIMS

By JERRY MARTIN

NEIGHBORHOOD
from THE SIMS

By JERRY MARTIN

Brisk Jazz Waltz

NOW ENTERING
from THE SIMS

By MARC RUSSO

SIM HEAVEN
from THE SIMS 2

By MARK MOTHERSBAUGH

SIM BUILDER
from THE SIMS 2

By MARK MOTHERSBAUGH

SIM TIME SIM PLACE

from THE SIMS 2

By MARK MOTHERSBAUGH

SIMS HEARTBEAT

from THE SIMS 2

By MARK MOTHERSBAUGH

THE SIMS THEME

from THE SIMS 3

By STEVE JABLONSKY

SIMULATION
THE SIMS 2

By MARK MOTHERSBAUGH

THE SIMS 2 THEME

from THE SIMS 2

By MARK MOTHERSBAUGH

SUL SUL
from THE SIMS 4

By ILAN ESHKERI

Driving

UNDER CONSTRUCTION

from THE SIMS

By JERRY MARTIN

YOUR FAVORITE MUSIC
ARRANGED FOR PIANO SOLO

    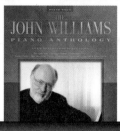 

ARTIST, COMPOSER, TV & MOVIE SONGBOOKS

**Adele for Piano Solo –
3rd Edition**
00820186

The Beatles Piano Solo
00294023

**A Charlie Brown
Christmas**
00313176

**Paul Cardall –
The Hymns Collection**
00295925

Coldplay for Piano Solo
00307637

**Selections from
Final Fantasy**
00148699

**Alexis Ffrench – The
Sheet Music Collection**
00345258

Game of Thrones
00199166

Hamilton
00354612

**Hillsong Worship
Favorites**
00303164

How to Train Your Dragon
00138210

Elton John Collection
00306040

La La Land
00283691

John Legend Collection
00233195

Les Misérables
00290271

Little Women
00338470

Outlander: The Series
00254460

**The Peanuts®
Illustrated Songbook**
00313178

**Astor Piazzolla –
Piano Collection**
00285510

**Pirates of the Caribbean –
Curse of the Black Pearl**
00313256

Pride & Prejudice
00313327

Queen
00289784

John Williams Anthology
00194555

George Winston Piano Solos
00306822

 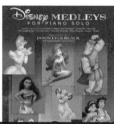   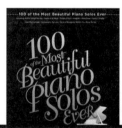 

MIXED COLLECTIONS

**Beautiful Piano
Instrumentals**
00149926

**Best Jazz
Piano Solos Ever**
00312079

**Big Book of
Classical Music**
00310508

Big Book of Ragtime Piano
00311749

Christmas Medleys
00350572

Disney Medleys
00242588

Disney Piano Solos
00313128

Favorite Pop Piano Solos
00312523

Great Piano Solos
00311273

**The Greatest Video
Game Music**
00201767

Most Relaxing Songs
00233879

**Movie Themes
Budget Book**
00289137

**100 of the Most Beautiful
Piano Solos Ever**
00102787

100 Movie Songs
00102804

Peaceful Piano Solos
00286009

**Piano Solos for
All Occasions**
00310964

Sunday Solos for Piano
00311272

Top Hits for Piano Solo
00294635

HAL•LEONARD®
View songlists online and order from your
favorite music retailer at
halleonard.com